CASSIE IS A GIRAFFE

CASSANDRA GAISFORD

Blue
Giraffe

CONTENTS

About the Transformational Super Kids Series   v
Praise for The Transformational Super Kids
Series   vii

Chapter 1   1
Chapter 2   3
Chapter 3   5
Chapter 4   7
Chapter 5   9
Chapter 6   11
Chapter 7   13
Chapter 8   15
Chapter 9   17
Chapter 10   19
Chapter 11   21
Chapter 12   23
Chapter 13   25
Chapter 14   27
Chapter 15   29
Chapter 16   31
Chapter 17   33
Chapter 18   35
Chapter 19   37
Author's Note   39
Also by The Author   45
Stay In Touch   47
Acknowledgements   49

Please Leave a Review   51

EXCERPT: LULU IS A BLACK
SHEEP

Chapter 1   55
Chapter 2   57
Chapter 3   59
Did you enjoy this excerpt?   61

Copyright   63

ABOUT THE TRANSFORMATIONAL
SUPER KIDS SERIES

From the bestselling author of *The Little Princess* comes a brilliant new series, *Transformational Super Kid*s.

These modern-day heroes and heroines tackle modern-day problems with the passion and gusto of warriors.

They defeat cruel critics, they slay savage self-esteem demons, and they show people—jealous of their kindness, talent, and beauty—that their biggest superpower is staying true to themselves.

Suitable for 'kids' of all ages—aren't we all still children at heart?

PRAISE FOR THE
TRANSFORMATIONAL SUPER KIDS
SERIES

"A Wonderful Little Helper for Self-esteem and to combat the effects of bullying...

"*Cassie is a Giraffe* is a lovely story told in a whimsical manner that will alleviate the effects of nasty taunts and meanness by others. It is a story of how Cassie the Giraffe recovered her sense of self and found a loving other who gave her strength to see that the taunts said so much more about the taunt-er, the power of love building self-worth, self-acceptance, and genuine love and support. A story for any age."

~ Catherine Sloan, Therapist

"Courageous, compassionate and inspiring...
I am a Midlife Coach, which means I help women find their moxie to do what they might not have done in the first half of their lives...Courage is more than just standing up for yourself or doing hard things—it's doing so with compassion. Little Hannah is courageous, compassionate, talented and inspiring!

"Such a powerful message....
This is a splendid little book for any person aspiring to reach another level. It has such a powerful message: Never, ever listen to anyone who steals your light. Cassandra is a shining example of turning every situation, including setbacks, into learning and growing opportunities.

As one who has taken advantage of the wisdom, knowledge, and ability of Cassandra to communicate over a number of years, I would encourage you to read this book thoroughly & think deeply about your own situation.

"Very uplifting and inspiring...
I love everything Cassandra writes, the queen of uplifting inspiration!"

Once upon a time in a small, hilly land lived a giraffe called Cassie. Cassie was tall. Tall. Tall. But she wanted to be small. Small. Small.

Cassie didn't want people to look at her. She didn't want to be seen. She didn't want to taunt her that she was being a queen.

Because everywhere that Cassie went people were mean. Mean. Mean.

2

"You think you're taller than us," the hill people spat. "But you're not."

"You think your spots are beautiful. But they're not."

"Why do you always wear dresses?" a girl in black shorts snapped.

"Are you trying to show off? You think you're hot. But you're not."

Cassie's face grew red. Red. Red.
She felt bad. Bad. Bad.
She felt sad. Sad. Sad.

Why couldn't people be glad? She didn't think about being taller. She didn't think about her spots. She didn't think she was better than anyone else.

Cassie was just being herself.

4

H er heart was huge.
      She had so much love.
  She loved everyone and everything.
  She loved the birds and the trees, the wind and the breeze.

S he even loved the mean people.

Why don't they love me back, she wondered. There's something wrong with me, she told herself. Maybe I'm a hard person to love.

Cassie studied her feet. Her second toe wasn't like other kids. It was longer than the first.

She looked at her hands. The left hand wanted to lead, to write, to paint with delight. But her mother fixed that.

Whack! Whack! Whack!

She was now right handed But she still wasn't like everyone else.

7

She looked at her legs. They were long and thin.

But she couldn't help that. Where could she possibly begin?

Her heart was huge. She felt too much. She felt everyone's pain. She felt everyone's anger. She felt their sorrow too.

"You're too sensitive. You need to toughen up," people shouted.

"Don't stick your neck out. Don't stand out. Don't make us look small," they jeered.

"I want to change everything about me," Cassie told her friend, Lulu, the black sheep. "I want to change my toes, my nose, my legs, my freckles—I want to lose my spots. I don't want to be a giraffe."

"What do you want to be?" asked Lulu.

"I want to be a mouse."

"A mouse! Why would you want to be a boring, teeny, weeny mouse?"

"I don't want to be me. Mice are small. Mice are quiet. Mice are safest. Mice can hide in tiny, teeny, weeny places."

C assie tried to be a mouse.

    Out went the pink dresses with white spots. In came beige. Lots and lots of boring beige.

"Don't feel. Don't care. Don't cry," she told herself. "Be a rock," she told her heart. "And you'll be made."

B ut nothing worked. She still stood out.

"Why can't I be like everyone else?" she asked Lulu. "Why is it so hard to be a mouse?"

"You're asking the sun to be the rain," Lulu said. "The sun doesn't stop shining so it won't feel pain. The sun shines anyway. It shines in the wind. It shines in the rain. It shines on the people who always complain: 'You're too hot. You're too bright. Nothing you do is ever right.' On and on they moan—with zero, zip, zeltch gratitude."

"Learn from the sun. Shine. Rise brilliantly. Learn from the sun to be soft yet strong. Learn from the sun to sing your song—no matter what's going wrong," Lulu said. "The sun always gets blamed. But it doesn't complain. The sun is the sun. And you, Cassie, are you. You are not a mouse. You are a giraffe."

Cassie looked up at the sun hidden from sight. The sun didn't shout, "Look at me. Look at me. Look at me. I am the sun. See how clever I can be."

The sun didn't try to be a bicycle, or a train, or a rocket.

The sun didn't try to be a mouse.

The sun was like Cassie—it was just being itself strong and proud and bright.

The sun wasn't sad when the clouds blocked its light. The sun shone anyway.

"The sun is happy just to 'be' isn't she?" she told Lulu.

"The sun is the sun and that's the fun!" Lulu said. "There is only one sun. The sun is herself. She loves and accepts her uniqueness. She shares her light. She shared her warmth. She shares her love."

"Where would we be if the sun stopped being the sun?" Lulu asked.

"The world would be black. The world would be cold. The world would be yuk. Yuk! Yuk!," Cassie said.

"If there were no giraffes where would we be?" Lulu asked.

"There would be no me," Cassie said. "But what can I do, Lulu? I don't want to stand out. I don't want to be seen. I don't want people to be mean, mean, mean."

"Just be a giraffe."

"Be who you are. Stand tall. Stand bright. Reach for the light," Lulu said. "Go on. Do it now. Reach for the sun. Reach for the stars."

17

Cassie stretched her legs. It felt so good. It felt so free.
Cassie stretched her neck. The pain released. The knots ceased.

Cassie reached for the sun. The stars. The sky.

"I feel great. I feel free. I feel like me. Me! Me!
How clever you are, Lulu, telling me to be free to be me."

"Once upon a time, people were mean to me, too," Lulu
said. They were cold, critical, and constantly put me down. I
soon learned that mean people will always want you to
change. But when you do, it's never enough. because the truth
is they don't like themselves. They don't like lots of stuff. It's
not us but them that needs to change."

"I'm not a car.
I'm not a house.
And I'm definitely not a mouse.

I'm Cassie. Cassie is a big, tall, spotted giraffe. I was born to stand out," she said, happily. "I've got to shine like the sun. I've got to shine in the wind, and the rain, and the hurricanes. I've got to keep being me."

* * * THE END * * *

AUTHOR'S NOTE

Here's something you may not know. Less than 14 percent of the population has a longer second toe. The numbers are similar for left-handed people too. Leonardo da Vinci was left-handed and he had a longer second toe too. He was bullied by friends and family and struggled a lot. But he had so many brilliant successes too. Some people are born to stand apart. Some people have to have the courage of a lion, and the grace of a giraffe to be who the are.

I hope reading this story has encouraged and empowered you to be you all the way through—from your toes to the sun and back. If we allow it...people, even well meaning people, can hold us back and bring us down. But within our own hearts and minds we have the power to rise above all that. The choice is always ours to make.

Sometimes you need a little more help than a book can give. Like I once did, perhaps you need the help of a skilled therapist to be free to you.

Therapy needn't be gloomy. A lot of healthy healing can be achieved using playfulness and fun. Personally and professionally I believe in magic and the power of beauty, joy, love, purpose, and creativity to transform peoples' lives. These are also scientifically-validated tools that enhance spiritual health and aid recovery.

Creativity in its various guises is a natural antidote to stress, anxiety, and depression, which explains why art therapy is such a potent and popular tool. Art therapy is a form of experiential therapy, an approach to recovery and healing that addresses emotional and spiritual needs through creative or physical activity. People don't need to have a background in the arts or any artistic talent to participate. They need only to be open to experiencing and engaging actively to benefit.

I have trained in a technique called <u>Interactive Drawing Therapy</u> and have found it to be an incredible tool in my own life and in my sessions with others. The simplest of drawings, a line, a colour, a scrawled phrase or word can powerfully access parts of the psyche we often repress, bringing unhelpful subconscious belief to light. In an alchemical process, wounds are spun into gold.

When I first trained in Interactive Drawing Therapy the teacher asked for a volunteer. No hands were raised so he picked me. What harm could it do, I thought, being as skilled as I was at keeping a lid firmly on my feelings.

"Draw an animal," he said.

Sure, I thought. Great. Harmless. I drew a giraffe.

"Put some colour on the page," the teacher gently guided.

My giraffe became pink with green, purple and yellow spots. What fun I thought.

"Where is she?" the teacher asked. "Draw this on the page."

I drew large grey and black rectangles, symbolising office blocks, cars belching smoke, and a road, not unlike Lambton

Quay, in Wellington, New Zealand where I went to work in a job I hated every weekday.

"Put some words on the page," the teacher whispered.

"She doesn't want to stand out."

And then it dawned on me, just as the words slipped onto the page. That giraffe was me. And the fact was I did stand out—naturally. I had always been different. And I had struggled unsuccessfully to belong.

"She can't help but stand out," my tutor affirmed. "It's who she is."

For me, this awareness was so new, so potent, so transformative, that I knew instantly there was work to do. I began to understand the deep social anxiety I had felt as a child and carried with me through adolescence—and with it the drinking and reckless behaviour I had adopted to belong, to bolster the confidence I never felt, to hide the discomfort of living in my own skin.

I'm glad to say, I now love the freedom of being my true, authentic self—spots and all!

I hope, having read this story, that you'll love being you, too.

audio notice

Cassie is a Giraffe **will soon be available as an audiobook for your listening enjoyment. Check out a free sample or grab your copy from your favourite online retailer.**

DEDICATION

For all the people who love my joy
who share their dreams with me,
and have achieved amazing feats.

Thank you for inspiring me.

ALSO BY THE AUTHOR

Stories and Fairytales

The Little Princess
I Have to Grow
The Little Boy Who Cried
The Little Princess Can Fly
Lulu is a Black Sheep
Jojo Lost Her Confidence
Why Doesn't Mummy Love Me?

Non-fiction Self-Empowerment Books

Mid-Life Career Rescue

How to Find Your Passion and Purpose

Bounce: Overcoming Adversity, Building Resilience and Finding Joy

Anxiety Rescue: How to Overcome Anxiety, Panic, and Stress and Reclaim Joy

Boost Your Self-Esteem and Confidence

No! Why 'No' is the New 'Yes'

More of Cassandra's practical and inspiring books on a range of life-enhancing topics can be found on her website (www. cassandragaisford.com) and her author page at all good online bookstores.

STAY IN TOUCH

Continue To Be Supported, Encouraged, and Inspired

www.thejoyfulartist.co.nz
https://www.facebook.com/CGTheJoyfulArtist/
https://www.instagram.com/the_joyful_artiste/
www.youtube.com/cassandragaisfordnz
https://www.thejoyfulartist.co.nz/category/blog/
https://www.thejoyfulartist.co.nz/book-collections/
www.tiktok.com/@cassandrathejoyfulartist

NEWSLETTERS

For inspiring tools and helpful tips, subscribe to Cassandra's free newsletters. **Sign up now and receive a free eBook — find your passion and purpose!** http://eepurl.com/bEArfT

Follow me on BookBub (https://www.bookbub.com/profile/cassandra-gaisford) and be the first to know about my new releases and giveaways

ACKNOWLEDGEMENTS

My daughter, Hannah—I wish for you everything that your heart desires. Without you, I doubt I would ever have accomplished all the things I have in my life. And I never would have written this book!

Freya and Finlay Wells, my beautiful niece and nephew, thank you so much for designing my logo for Blue Giraffe Publishing—and for helping my books fly. You were both under six-years of age at the time and already born with such great spirit.

As Coco Chanel once said, "If you were born without wings, do nothing to prevent them from growing."

Thank you.

PLEASE LEAVE A REVIEW

Word of mouth is the most powerful marketing force in the universe. If you found this book useful, I'd appreciate you rating this book and leaving a review. You don't have to say much—just a few words about how the book helped you learn something new or made you feel.

"Your books are a fantastic resource and until now I never even thought to write a review. Going forward I will be reviewing more books. So many great ones out there and I want to support the amazing people that write them."
Great reviews help people find good books.

Thank you so much! I appreciate you!

PS: If you enjoyed this book, do me a small favour to help spread the word about it and share on Facebook, Twitter and other social networks.

EXCERPT: LULU IS A BLACK SHEEP

1

Once upon a time, there was a little black sheep. Her hair was black as coal.

And everything that Lulu did her family disapproved.

They shamed Lulu to her face.

They criticised her behind her back.

They were cold, and critical, and constantly put her down.

And they always looked at her with a heavy, dark, frown.

L ulu tried to make them love her.

Lulu tried to make them happy.

Lulu tried to please them.

She tried to be like the rest of the flock.

She tried to be a little white sheep.

Here a baaaa. There a baaaa. Everywhere a baaaa. Baaaa!

But what she really wanted to say was "Yippee! Wow-wee! All the things we can be!"

But she kept her mouth shut.

She tried to make her fleece go white.

She tried to come out of the shadows.

But every time Lulu did, her family bellowed. And they threw her back.

"Why are you being mean to me?" she asked.

"There's something wrong with you," they snapped.

3

One night when Lulu woke up she felt lonely and sad. She sat in the darkness because the black and the stillness always made her feel glad.

Night-time, when everyone else was in bed, was the time she loved best.

Suddenly Lulu heard a shrill, sharp, sound.

Squark! Squark! Squark!

She ran to the window and saw a funny looking bird in the bush. She went for a walk in her pyjamas and stumbled upon a nest.

"Who are you? Lulu asked.

"I'm a kiwi," the little bird replied.

"Birds are supposed to fly," Lulu said.

"I don't want to be like other birds," the kiwi said.

DID YOU ENJOY THIS EXCERPT?

Follow Your Own Truth. Cherish Who You Are.

When Lulu's family tells her that she doesn't belong, she thinks she's all alone. Until the Kiwi in black jumps out from the night bringing with her wisdom, wonder, and surprise!

"Delightful and uplifting. . .
Lulu is a black sheep is a delightful and empowering story for our times! Uplifting messages are woven throughout. A feel-good story most will relate to, especially grown ups! Another one to add to your collection of Cassandra's self-empowerment books! Thank you Cassandra! Delightful and uplifting!"
~ Heather Dodge

Lulu is a Black Sheep is an inspiring story and personal development guide for girls with themes on self-esteem and resilience.

Available in Audio, Hardback, eBook and Paperback from all great online retailers.

COPYRIGHT

rendering professional advice or services to the individual reader. The ideas, procedures, and suggestions contained in this book are not intended as a substitute for psychotherapy, counseling, or consulting with your physician.

The intent of the author is only to offer information of a general nature to help you in your quest for emotional, physical, and spiritual well-being.

Any use of information in this book is at the reader's discretion and risk. Neither the author nor the publisher can be held responsible for any loss, claim, or damage arising out of the use or misuse of the suggestions made, the failure to take medical advice, or for any material on third-party websites.

First published by Blue Giraffe Publishing 2020

ISBN PRINT: 978-1-99-002054-4
ISBN EBOOK: 978-1-99-002052-0
ISBN HARDBACK: 978-1-99-002055-1
ISBN AUDIO: 978-1-99-002053-7